AF448923

Also By Tevin Curtis Ryan Dubé

Book Of The Enlightened One

Amen: A Great Light Within Divine Darkness

The Mystery Behind Life, Death and Resurrection

A Silent Truth

SELF

Psalms From A New King David

Attract Abundance; Learn How To Live Abundantly

The Universal Key

Tevin C. R. Dubé

ISBN: 978-976-96334-4-5

Publishers Note

Tevin Curtis Ryan Dubé

Trinidad and Tobago

Email: tevindube@yahoo.com

Facebook Page –Tevin 'Mystical' Dube

Instagram – mystical_dube

Twitter – @mysticaldube

Cover Design by Tevin C. R. Dubé

& Vector Glifs Studio

CONTENTS

Section One

9

once you are in possession of this key

you become one with all of infinity

One

Profoundly Rhetoric

Are we breathing the air or is it the air that is breathing us?

Is the air invisible to us or are we invisible to the air?

Why do we feel the wind's touch but still cannot feel it with our perceived sense of touch?

Or is that when the wind blows it is actually feeling us?

Do we actually dream as we sleep or is it sleep that is actually dreaming about us?

Does death bring an end to the flesh or does the flesh bring the end of death as it dies?

It seems like we are living to die but are we actually dying in order to live?

Are we truly experiencing Life or is this existence actually the process of death?

We know we all came from our mother's womb but what if we are still developing within another womb?

What if our concept of time is what birthed the ideology of life and decay?

What if every answer you receive is yet still another major question left unanswered?

The rhetoric of Life is when you think you have it all figured out, you haven't figured out anything at all.

Two

Glimpses of Seeing The Unseen

Some of us have young bodies but are in possession of an ancient spirit.

It is foolish to believe that a simple child cannot teach thee.

"You still don't understand life with your little self?!" a seven-year-old randomly asked me.

"No…can you teach me?" With great intrigue, I responded.

Wondering what spirit could have possibly swayed this little seedling to bring forth such a request of me.

With a little pause, he then said to me, "Life is like a human being."

And with that, he both astounded and astonished me.

Not that I didn't know, but it was in the way this natural mystic had reminded me.

Bob Marley said, "Knowledge isn't free, you have to pay attention."

A bunch of old souls for many are reincarnated.

A bunch of divinity for a few is incarnated.

How would you love to be treated as a human being?

This little insight will train you how to deal with Life.

For even though we are living life, Life is a being still living and experiencing a life all on its own.

Three

The Key That Unlocks

A simple question is the key that unlocks a wealth of knowledge.

Why am I not allowed to question God?

Then it is a great contradiction to "Free Will."

Yet still, the many unanswered questions have a slow burn deep within.

If God took six days to create Heaven and Earth;

Then how did it take that same God forty days and 40 nights to give Moses only the Ten Commandments?

Ten Commandments that were never scribed by Moses at first, but carved by the finger of God!

One thing alone could have transpired;

Who? What? Why? When? How?—only question after question.

"Test every spirit whether it is of God or not, for there are many false prophets in the Earth."

Isn't it written in 1st John 4:1?

To test the validity of something is for it to make proof of itself.

For a man to make proof of himself, he must be equipped with wisdom.

And to prove that one is in possession of such is as a result of questions being presented.

Many false prophets tell you to never question not just God but the Divine within.

If God is omniscient, all-knowing and knowing all things;

Then automatically it means that you can ask freely.

Life was always meant to be lived freely.

Yet institutions now dominate us not just physically but mentally.

The answer to every question abides with that which is within your possession internally.

When you ask, listen carefully to that silent voice that speaks loudly within.

Four

Indomitable

If I were created in the image of God,

Then why am I being forced to try and find God?

You see, I've looked for God in so many places,

I tasted a taste on my tongue that was still tasteless.

I've seen the face of a God that is still faceless.

I've been exploring the globe.

As I searched through the world

I even left this place

As I ventured out into space

As I questioned and searched within my mind

Penetrating the illusion of time

An uphill battle or a mountainous climb

It's like searching for a bright light while the sun still shines

The Universal Key

Then I realised that I was created in the image of God

I then became still and began to find God

I became estranged from the main place as I
explored other strange places.

The tasteless taste on my tongue no longer remained
tasteless.

I swapped my vision from only looking into the world

And recognised the need to start looking into my
own soul

Great answers were awaiting me, like 'Lo and behold'

Five

Saving Grace

It is not always easy to do

But sometimes, to rescue someone

You have to be willing to step into their fantasy

And bring them back to reality using balance.

To save a drowning man

The lifeguard cannot be afraid to get wet.

Going within can appear to be a lonely and scary thing

But it is imperative for you to know

That's when it all boils down in the end

You are already in possession of the power to save your own soul.

Section Two

Six

Open Eyes Doesn't Always See

You want to know why spirituality is important!

No matter the amount of physical possessions you accumulate

It is all still left behind as the spiritual journey continues.

I am not saying to not seek that which is physical

But I beg, please don't get lost in the pursuit.

There will always be chaos if the tail wags the head.

The moment you stop running is the very moment you've won.

Seven

The Master Architect

What if this is all just an illusion?

An illusion necessary for the construction of a personal euphoria

One filled with idealistic people and perceptions.

What if all the imperfections of this world are the aid necessary for such a grand architecture?

One that can only be designed within a mind full of escapes and not easily be distracted;

By fears, doubts and disbelief

A mind free to imagine without bounds

After all, the vastness of space still lies within the mind.

So the kingdom of such a heaven can only be accessed internally.

What if our temporal joys established are to serve as reminders...

Of that which is awaiting beyond the illusions of all our pains felt?

The Universal Key

What if the endurance of this existence is to build
such to fly off to in the end?

Construct well!

But while we're here, dare to dream big

Learn to master manifesting and live abundantly.

Radiate and vibrate at higher frequencies

For Legacy is an eternal well,

So let us drink responsibly.

Eight

The Difference Between Spirit And Soul

As a flag flaps, it is the presence of the unseen wind.

It represents an element beyond the physical that yet binds our existence.

The swaying of the trees and the ruffling of the leaves,

The very freshness of the breeze is indicative to us human beings.

When the Breath of Life first entered through the nostrils,

Man became a living soul.

So, prior to that, he was nothing more than a motionless soul

But upon his initial breath, animation of the flesh sprang into being.

Spirit and Soul are both separate entities,

The Universal Key

The Spirit is the representation of the primary principle, unseen

That yet still consists of the very air we breathe.

Therefore, the body in motion is made unto the likeness of a flag representation.

A physical representation that is proof of the spiritual

With both combined, it signifies a divine type of union.

It is now the manifestation of the Spirit being human,

Yet the living souls of men as a collective are to experience emotions as a body in motion.

So collectively we are called the human being manifestation.

Nine

Higher Cognitive Perspective

There is a pure sense of consciousness at work

In the development of a baby yet still unconscious.

Consciousness is always conscious of itself

For even though we were unconscious, consciousness was natural in that we still naturally grew into consciousness.

How does a baby know how to automatically breathe?

How do they know to suck from the first time they are breastfed?

There is something very real about the unseen.

Seek ye first the kingdom that is within, and everything shall be added unto thee.

Through what medium does consciousness truly flow into our being?

What if we are naturally projecting our consciousness from a different plain?

How do we know if we have access to a library that is Universal?

One where we can log in spiritually to gain any kind of experience!

What if some of us are from a different time zone and have access to this current ripple in time?

We know that this existence is a test, but what exam are we specifically trying to ace?

And what are the prices and rewards associated?

What if the test is that if you can make it here, you can make it anywhere?

Not just anywhere physically, but spiritually universally.

What if the true plane we exist upon is a fundamental requirement for higher development?

What if this is a training ground like the barracks to attain higher ranks?

Whatever it may be, consciousness will forever be conscious indeed.

Ten

The Contrast

One helps you to transcend to a higher mental state, and the other to constantly rearrange the cubicle spacing of the mind.

Spirituality is to become an explorer.

While religion is engineered to establish settlers

It is like they who know it have a whole wide world to explore out there

But still cannot see beyond the village gates.

One enables you to become more endearing as it seeks to continuously free up the dome of your mind.

While the other has become systematically designed to rule by cowing the mind into a comfort zone, in fear of the unknown

It is like those who know about the vastness of space filled with endless galaxies.

And still believe that the only existing intelligent species is that of human beings.

Think of spirituality as the entire ocean, and we are the fish swimming in the sea.

Religion is like placing a fish tank in the sea with fish swimming within, thinking they are free.

A shark in a fish tank will never grow beyond its environment.

Yet the same shark in the sea grows beyond its limits.

It is like the planting of the same tree;

One in a pot and the other within fertile earth

The latter will continuously grow to maximum capacity

While the former must adapt to the confines of not being able to properly spread its roots.

Spirituality is the key ingredient indeed.

Spirituality is the expression of a spirit that is free

For a bird can still fly within a cage

Yet still, it restricts its capabilities and fullest potentialities.

Eleven

The Temporal Container

The body is but a container that momentarily captures the essence of Life to be expressed uniquely. – Tevin C. R. Dubé

Being human is to actually experience a temporal trap.

If not, then explain why one is always in search of freedom.

We want to attain free expression of spirit

And be free from mental stresses and the limited constraints of the mind

And escape from emotional instability,

Be free to express sensuality and sexuality

And attain financial freedom and be free from prejudice and judgment

With the wish to roam the world freely

And escape all societal confines and incarceration that restrict freedom to be free.

The happiest people are often regarded as free-spirited

And when Life becomes too much, many ask to be free from it.

The many freedoms within Life are yet still temporal sustenance.

Whereas death may seem to be a permanent trap for the body

It is yet still the ultimate freedom expressed spiritually.

As the elderly pass on, often the cause is that of old age.

But old age represents the fact that their spirit now has no choice but to escape

For this prison sentence in the flesh was never meant to keep a spirit that is bound to be free eternally.

To experience emotions is to be a body in motion. Hence, the body is a prison sentence to the spirit in order for it to realise that true freedom has always been mental. – Tevin C. R. Dubé

We are already trapped in flesh, so the best gift you can give yourself is to be free mentally. – Tevin C. R. Dubé

Twelve

Who Are You?

In death, people consider that that person has left.

The body now becomes the remains, corpse, deceased and so forth.

Death makes people realise that the spirit makes the soul, and the soul gives character that makes the person.

Therefore, the true individual was never the body but that which can leave it behind at any time.

The problem with many is that they treat people according to the flesh and not the spiritual.

And it's sad that death does have to remind many of how shallow they have been with many while they are yet still alive.

Just like clothing is to cover the nakedness of the bare soul,

Is in the same manner, the body is the covering for the nakedness of one's spiritual entity.

That is the real embodiment of you being human as a human being.

Section Three

Thirteen

Time Reveals

Sometimes you have to stop trying so hard to get people to be involved in your life.

Because you have great intentions in mind for them, but cannot say just yet.

Don't force them because they are unable to see your visions and the true wealth of your thoughts through your consistent actions.

Let them go with ease.

Those deserving of it will come as a gentle breeze.

Some people have to look at you, your life and happiness from the outside.

So just let them be

Fourteen

Energy Vampires

Someone who constantly seeks you for comfort

Gains strength from your uplifting capabilities

Leaves you and depletes the strength you have given

And then randomly shows up again to regain strength from your positivity.

As you intake and filter their own negative perpetuation

It takes away from you greatly.

See these vampires for who they are and safeguard your energy.

Let your yea be yea, and your nay be nay.

Escape that loop and don't fall victim to that cycle.

Manage your empathy

Know when to feel and when not to.

Balance is fundamental, and sometimes you have to switch off for a while

And be inaccessible for your own sake.

The Universal Key

Rain doesn't fall every day,

Know your empathetic season.

Fifteen

True Treasure

You will stop "wanting" the love of others

To validate your importance

After you realise

That self-love is not only a "necessity"

But "priority"

Showing love is the greatest above all

But balance will teach you when to love from afar.

It is always good to like those who like you.

It is even better to genuinely love those who love you.

Such is a blessing because it will save you from breaking your own heart.

One day, you'll be desired by someone very special who is tailored to suit you.

They may not be the initial ones you desire

But you'll see that above your wants

That will be the one you need.

And with that newfound worth of yours,

Few will admire, aspire to achieve and appreciate it

While many will resent, regret, hate and envy it.

But gratitude will permanently establish it.

Treat others like options, and you too will become an option. Treat others like a priority, and you too will become a priority.

Affirmation:

I am not an option, nor do I ever want to be such in anyone's life. I am a priority because you always get what you give.

Sixteen

Single Parent

When Buju sang, "Consider how she makes it through the end of the day working so hard just to get paid... As a single parent, you know it's not easy playing the role of mom and dad."

Those words echoed deep within my soul back when I was a child. It was as if he had written those words specifically for me to hear them. It was more than heartfelt because it touched my soul and strummed a spiritual cord.

"Why do you look so dull and forsaken? I know that he's gone and your heart is broken. But we are still together. Mama, you never leave us at home alone, no."

Buju Banton's song entitled 'Single Parent' will always have a special place in my heart, for those words reflected the life my little household had been subjected to.

"So when mama spends her last and sends you to class, don't you ever play. It's a competitive world for low-budget people," Buju sang in 'Untold Stories' for the half has never been told.

I've always held my mother in the highest regard possible. Everything I do and continue to do is to be able to alleviate her from her constant toils.

I really never played as I went to class. I had to bear forth fruits as a payment for my single mother's labours; she had to endure.

Even though I was rejected at first, I would go on to graduate as the top student in my high school. I pursued my education because of Mama.

I had to achieve. For there was a time when I was graced by the Almighty in a dream, asking, "Do you want to remain with me in paradise for an eternity or go back on earth to fulfil your duties?"

I greatly contemplated remaining in that ineffable bliss, but I chose my single mother instead. I was so young, but numb, but for her, I stayed strong and continued to advance.

Always seeking new ideas to become her inevitable uplifting ensured the many blows I've felt. But my love for her made me to endure peculiar tortures.

I felt great pain every time my progress was deliberately interrupted. Nonchalant on the outside while managing great anguish within.

It hurt seeing my mother have to settle for next to nothing and be content with it. And to me, trying everything lawfully and morally to give her that ease and comfort gets overlooked and suppressed.

Because I set out to uplift her, the entire world would benefit simultaneously. I pour out my experiences through these pens to heal others, and I am yet to catch that break. But my spirit is determined.

Every so often, I would sit on the toilet listening to Buju Banton songs as a reminder. Silently, the tears would stream from my eyes as I visualise. Both of sadness and yet still giving me the strength and hope to carry on.

Even Sizzla songs 'Give Thanks' and 'Thank You Mama' would reassure me that I would be triumphant. I would soon kill many birds with the same stone. All the pain I've felt and the things I've endured shall never go in vain.

For I acknowledge my mother in all my ways. And I even proved this before the glory of the Most High Divine.

"For my destination is homeward bound. No forces try hold I down. Breaking chains have become the norm. I know I must get through no matter what ah go on." Buju sang in his 'Destiny' song.

Seventeen

The Perfect Crossroad

I don't need to have multiple relationships

To know who is for me and who is not

I don't need to have sex with every green light

To not know when to stop

I don't need to walk the same path as most usually
do.

Creating a new road will make you seem
disconnected from the crowd

But you will find exactly what you need

Because someone else is creating a new path as well

The perfect crossroad

Is that of Universal Alignment

Eighteen

The Virtuous Woman

A virtuous woman isn't only concerned about her self-image

And social status, all in an attempt to please the masses

And try to impress those she is not particularly fond of.

She is more concerned about sustainability

That will carry itself on for generations.

She is always ready and willing to build and invest

And establish a proper foundation for her offspring, present and future.

She knows how to keep a man and can easily distinguish

The boys walking around who are being disguised as men.

But most importantly, she knows how to speak life into him

And be the cause for extracting the king within him.

She knows her divine role in Life

And is not too independent to the point that she is out of balance

Rather, she knows the truth of interdependence.

She creates a home where there isn't autonomy.

There is no head and tail,

But there is a perfect sense of equity and rule

Just like the relationship between night and day.

Society's standards of beauty and relationship goals, she doesn't conform to.

Because she is intellectual beyond systematic programming

Looking good is just a bonus factor because her mind is already dressed well.

For she can easily sacrifice trivialities for the greater good

She always looks ahead and walks upright and strong in her integrity.

She has no time for gossip and stays clear of dragging down another.

Not everyone has access to her body and her music

Her divinity is perfection

Royalty in flesh, for she embodies the epitome of a queen

That awakened the goddess deep within.

Section Four

Nineteen

All-Knowing Or Knowing All

Having common sense is not important if common sense doesn't have you.

Intelligence has always existed as the very Source of pure consciousness.

Therefore, reasoning with wisdom, logic and innerstanding is a vital attribute that allows for an ever-open mind for any discussion.

One thing I cannot afford is cheap thoughts

And being around inexpensive minds

Being able to memorise words is a talent.

However, mastering the art of being able to break things down in a simplistic manner is a divine gift.

There are many who are educated but not edified.

There are those who are edifiers without education

And there are those who are in possession of both.

Twenty

Sublime Lines

Simplicity is the greatest attribute of all complexity

For through simplicity, great attention is paid to the fine details.

Every word uttered reveals how someone truly thinks

And the consistency of one's actions truly cements it.

Like someone who always wants to make a phone call

Trying to advantage the situation because another has free calls

There is no limit to the blatant ways of inconsiderate minds

Till one time I said profoundly, "You know that free calls aren't really free."

Faces now looking at me profusely, rhetorical

Someone still had to pay a fee before it became free.

There are many things in Life that are free that yet still isn't free.

For even though the air we breathe and our life-force are free

It came at a cost of our mothers' travailing in great pain and agony.

Yet it is a blessing to breathe, even though daily we live as sacrificial beings.

Life is all about simplicity. Allow me to better express such. No matter how many pairs of shoes you have, you can only wear one pair at a time.

– Tevin C. R. Dubé

Twenty-One

High-Spirited Individuals

The most high-spirited individuals are often the least judgmental.

There is a fine line between correction and embarrassment. Know exactly where you stand and where you would like to be placed.

Being childlike is a blessing, but thinking and acting childish as an adult is shameful unto a child's truly divine order.

One of the filthiest places on Earth can be found in the heart of the self-righteous and the mind of a vile and indiscriminate judger.

One of the purest and cleanest places to be found on the Earth is among the misunderstood, outcast and condemned in society.

Even though the most high-spirited individuals are often the least judgmental, it's because they are either their own worst judge, conditioned to feel judged, or have been judged, criticised and ostracised the most.

Twenty-Two

Domino Effect

Many come to me seeking answers to the many questions they ask.

Remember, behind every answer, a showed working is required to gain approval.

So if I give you an answer, remember that you're still required to do the necessary work to arrive at it for yourself.

Otherwise, you will leave yourself undone.

You are your own saviour

And experience will always be the greatest teacher.

Success is preceded by its tutor, Failure.

I am just here to enlighten you to become enlightened to enlighten another.

Enlightenment is for all to partake freely, but I cannot force anyone.

Section Five

Twenty-Three

A Prophet's Profit

How can a prophet be without profit, even though he has no profit, while still being a prophet?

A prophet is seldom without profit, even though he may not have profited while still being a prophet.

People tend to confuse a job with work. When you get paid for your time, that is a job you are conducting. But taking time to develop yourself is when you are truly at work. Finding balance will create a job you love from your work.

Therefore, a prophet can still have profit after profiting while still being a prophet. A true prophet will always be of divine profit unto people, whether he is able to profit from it or not.

Twenty-Four

Life's Passover

There are those who initially know the taste of sweetness, like sugar.

Then there are those who initially know the bitter taste of aloe.

When the latter tastes the sweetness of sugar,

What a sweet it is indeed!

The bitter taste of aloe is but a memory.

But when the bitterness of always tasting sweet strikes,

Diabetes is an everyday reminder of a painful reality.

See your life for what it actually is,

Accept it in that you may find that grand state of equilibrium.

Learn to stomach the bitter taste of your hardships,

For your sugar of triumph shall be the sweetest.

The Universal Key

Your honey of victory shall be pure nourishment

And the remembrance of days of bitter shall be your
Passover.

It shall be a great reminder to always express our
sincerest gratitude.

Easy street without balance generally has bitter
endings.

A life too easy only breeds mediocrity

And makes for an ungrateful heart and an egotistical
being

And a spirit that thirsts and starves from deprivation
of growth and the balance of humility

Twenty-Five

Life's Rhetoric

You must first learn about Life before you can live it. And only when you begin to live, do you start to learn Life.

You never truly live until you've experienced death. Yet as you live, you are made to constantly experience many deaths while still being alive.

Every stage of Life represents new growth. Every new growth represents both an ending and a new beginning.

And since death is a part of our experience, it too is symbolic of both an end and a fresh start.

Twenty-Six

The Key To Existence

Unlike the Source of All Existence, experience is our greatest teacher.

Through experience, knowledge is gained

And the more experience is attained, the more wisdom is forthwith, the more knowledge is gained.

And with the procurement of wisdom, the propitious one becomes not just at understanding but overstanding.

These three are the pillars of stability.

They are the balance of the Divine Trinity.

The wisest men that ever lived will attest to the fact that wisdom is better than Life.

He whosoever is in possession of such is bound to exist for an eternity.

His riches are to always exist forevermore.

Having knowledge, wisdom and understanding as a combination is to reveal the secret behind all of creation.

To innerstand is to yet still overstand.

To be in possession of the three is to be in possession of the key

Of the key

That is made to unlock all doors universally

Even spiritually, though physically.

The code can only be unlocked deep within your soul

For internally the secret is hidden waiting to be discovered and be revealed.

It is imperative for you to open your main eye to see that you must become the key because you already are.

It would make no sense to gain all the money in the world

And lack the knowledge about the true wealth existing within one's own soul.

Without wisdom, it will all be for nought.

For sad be the man who dies without knowledge and wisdom of the divine.

Not only is his wealth left for the inheritance of strangers

But his existence too shall become evanescent

And be buried by time to be lost for an eternity, and be forgotten by mortal minds.

Great is the man who holds the key

For even though death be for all, he shall never die

And even though all flesh falls, his spirit shall forever stand tall.

Great is he who finds this everlasting key as a temporal being

For he shall be one with the Source of all eternity

Section Six

Twenty-Seven

The Choice

In Life, you can either become inspired or become jealous.

Inspiration fills you up with light, whilst jealousy anchors you in darkness that poisons you from the inside out.

It is the darkness that makes the light to become illustrious.

Trying to block the light of another will only make you to become lost in your own darkness.

The true devil lies in the mind of the envious and the heart of the jealous.

Twenty-Eight

Outshine The Sun!

It is not wise to try and outshine the Sun on a sunny day.

It will only highlight your envy of the Sun's abundant rays.

The Sun has a time to shine just as much as the moon.

They both are great leaders who share equal rule.

Trying to outshine another when it's their time to shine

Will never diminish their glow

But your hidden actions will inevitably be exposed.

Jealousy will only make you become blinded to your own light

And eventually, such a one will become dim to others sight.

Twenty-Nine

Different Reflections

Always remember, a star never sees its own light

Neither does a planet get to see its own glow.

Your light is reflected through the reaction of others towards you

By the way, you shine towards them.

Some will be inspired and naturally flock to you

Some will wish to bask in your glow, and some may never even know.

Others will despise you for being you

Some will avoid and act blindly towards you

Because of it, but when things seem dark

Know that you are shining at your brightest

For darkness is always attracted to light

But it is upon the backs of darkness that light is made to travel further

It could never be tainted

So magnify yourself and shine brighter without fear.

Thirty

Untouched Essence

You can learn so much from the purity and innocence of kids.

It is so ironic that on Diwali night, I further recognised this.

A little girl shone a light from a torch upon the ground and told another to stomp it with their feet.

My consciousness was alerted and allowed me to capture this playful event.

I saw the little girls stomping as hard as they could to hurt it

Then a profound revelation came to me swiftly without thought.

No matter how much people try to fight your good

The one trying to trample your light will never feel good.

Futile attempts will leave them enervated and be put to rest.

They will only hurt themselves in the process of trying to touch an untouched essence.

The true source of your light could never be disturbed

For whatever it casts itself upon cannot help but to experience it.

Thirty-One

The Door To Endless Possibilities

No matter how many doors get shut on you in your life

Never slam the main door that resides mentally within your mind.

The door to limitless possibilities resides within the subconscious mind

Of those who dare to ceaselessly believe in themselves

And work in tandem with imagination; the key

Where you will have unlimited access to create any reality of your choosing.

So when one door closes

Leave gracefully without resistance or force

And upon your return

Make sure you buy that entire building

And remove that door.

Only you can shut yourself out from the door of endless possibilities.

Section Seven

Thirty-Two

Handouts

Handouts are like cocaine.

It gives you a momentary high

A brief period of numbness felt by temporal relief

But as soon as it wears off,

You can be scampering for your next fix

Another temporal source of uplifting.

Never put a price on your integrity

Because it would make you become an addict

And indebted to whoever may purchase it.

Dig your own pond and breed your own fish

Create your own opportunities to fill your own dish.

Thirty-Three

So Close Yet Still So Far

I know you can lead a horse to water, but you cannot force it to drink.

But what happens when you reach to a waterfall

And was intentionally hindered after earning the right to drink from it?

It's like an unhappy salesman tasked with selling happiness

And he himself could never earn enough to purchase it.

I've experienced that unhappy salesman personally.

I've felt that great thirst in the presence of pristine water.

 So close, but yet still so far

Only in darkness, the light of a star becomes visible and is made to travel farther.

It is hard to first work and return with an empty hand.

Hard lessons truly test the integrity and character of a trying man who is more than worthy.

It's hard to accept that this is truly a temporal existence

In that, these trials can test you so much that you wish to forfeit your very breath.

Though heartbreaking, the inheritance of wisdom is rich and eternal forever.

Thirty-Four

Unsung Apologies

A man's subconscious mind can be his best friend or his own worst enemy.

Learn to accept the sorries that will never be spoken. It's hard for many to say sorry, but it is most difficult to please humans all the same. Damn if you do, damn if you don't.

Many choose to say sorry indirectly through acts consistently rather than words. Pay attention to the details in little actions. For it is better to prove you're sorry through actions consistent than repetition of vain words.

But most times we become too blinded to see by our own anger, biases, prejudices and lust to see others hurting for their wrongs.

A heavy conscience is the greatest burden to carry. No man can successfully escape it for as long as he is alive, but he can master it by learning to take full control of his mind.

Not because you never see your foes crying doesn't mean that they aren't hurting. Guilt and regret are the deadliest assassins of the mind, courtesy of the ever-subconscious reminder. Be at peace within yourself and know this truth. Time will gently sing to you the silent tunes of unsung apologies.

Thirty-Five

Couch

Through it all, you were the only one who provided me comfort.

The weight of me you felt constantly

As I lay with the burdens of a heavy heart

And a mind weary, mentally depleted and exhausted.

I know if you could talk, you would attest to the things I've felt.

As my spirit sank deep within my soul

I became heavy with depression.

I hate that loneliness always had to be my friend.

O couch, help me to bear my burdens.

As I am now made to lie upon you ceaselessly for many days and nights

I've tried and tried, and Life seems to hate my every effort made.

The Universal Key

It is always one thing to the next.

Every time I make a little progress, my momentum is
constantly thwarted.

What vendetta is always meted out to me?

I am becoming loathsome of my constant ordeals
measured out to me.

Take away this curse from me if you can, O couch.

You're the only one holding me up in this sunken
place.

Your own people can prove to be your own worst
enemy.

When you're in a position of power, you help!

When you can be a blessing don't choose to be a
curse for your punishment shall be the worst.

Couch, you saw my tears

You felt my pain

You felt my weight

Three hundred sixty-five days, you became my scale.

I kept trying and trying

But to no avail

I've failed and failed.

Couch, I am here because of envy and jealousy

I am here because I am too ambitious

I am here because my light was intimidating

I am here because of feigned lips and deceitful hearts

It has been 2 years now, and I am still here on the couch.

Oh, couch, you have witnessed me in my cocoon of darkness.

You saw the dimming of my light suppressed by silent stress.

Induced by blatant fight-downs I've always had to face.

I humbled myself as I was technically spat upon with malicious disgrace.

I was only trying to find a place where I belonged and establish a little happiness of my own.

The books I wrote were the new identity I've created humbly.

To identify this nonentity who always felt like a
nobody.

Finally, I thought I saw a light at the end of this long
tunnel.

Only for my train to be derailed through false hope
and assurance

How much more must I endure to be made approved
to the Universe, O couch?

Couch, you are very strong

To hold up this burden and not fall

Even though when I felt like all my strength had gone

Upon you, I found meditation by learning to be still.

Now, through the pandemic of COVID-19, I am calm
and made strong

Sitting yet standing tall in mind, writing these lines;

Oh, couch, you never let me fall

Seeing me emerge anew through this trying
metamorphosis of mines

Thirty-Six

Highest Disappointment

O merciful Divine, let my words be acceptable unto Thee;

Just like Job when he was sorely afflicted and tormented.

For I too am made to be torn and conflicted

And greatly troubled and tormented.

My heart is in constant despair, and I am melancholy.

I am disappointed with Life and how things keep turning out.

I can't even hold back my tears as I say these words to You.

I dedicate all that I do just for You

And I can't help but feel disappointed

Because in You I do hope all the day long, for what choice do I have?

I put all my trust in You, and years of nothing but stagnation.

I am tired of always having to see things from a higher perspective.

Can things go my way for once?

No hiccups, no hurt, no pain, no disappointments, no deceitfulness.

Is it too hard to just experience this once and for all?

I am disappointed in You Most High.

Because it is You who deliberately keeps failing me.

How long must I endure all the things I am constantly made to feel?

How long must I come before You with the same plight?

I hate begging, and I am starting to feel as if I am doing such.

That is why I stopped saying my prayers.

I do work hard, and I am rewarded with sore disappointment each time.

I look forward to You and I can't help but to feel let down.

You let me down the greatest and disappoint me the most.

I hoped in You more than that of men who could have made things happen.

Everything that happened to me, it is You who allowed it.

Please understand that I still have emotions, so feel my pain.

I asked of Thee permission to say what I have to say

Because I cannot lie to myself

And for that, I could never lie to You Most High Divine.

For even though I am let down

I know I am made to feel disappointed in You because of You and by You.

Yet still I have no choice but to look forward to You.

I am disappointed, but still haven't lost my faith and hope in You completely, O Divine.

I thought you were finally giving me my breakthrough

So close but yet still so far, I trusted You wholeheartedly, and I felt like You had abandoned me.

Your hand is too heavy upon me.

I now see the difference between being called and chosen.

For he who is called still has a choice

But he who is chosen is a far cry from being called along the way.

I need sustenance, for I am made to be dull

I need what is owed unto me

I need all the great things I've earned that were denied to me.

I've sacrificed my all unto the honour of You. Must I now beg of You bread?

Stop disappointing me because I know it is all You.

Stop letting me down in sore disappointment.

Haven't I learned enough tough lessons as it is to finally be granted my right to feel free?

Bitter has always been the taste of sweetness on my tongue.

Tevin C. R. Dubé

I am weary, O Divine

I am worthy, and You know this.

Grant unto me all my heart's desires

So that I may fulfil all my desires unto Thee

You alone know my heart, and You know that it is pure.

I know You are pleased with me because my actions still answer Your calls when I choose not to speak.

Hear me now as I call.

The only thing I can offer is my honesty and brokenness, may it be acceptable unto Thee.

O Almighty, help me to rule my destiny.

Thirty-Seven

Divine Detours

While sailing through Life,

Some will derail and hinder you

From boarding certain voyages

In attempts for you never reach your destination.

But sometimes being tossed off that ship

Were meant to save you from sinking with it

All shall be well and fine

And even though it may greatly hurt

You will never be late

But will still arrive alive

And be even greater all in divine time.

Thirty-Eight

The Everlasting Fruit

People will almost only celebrate you for as long as you're in season.

But the real ones will cherish and preserve you like fruits to be enjoyed even when you are no longer being fruitful and in season.

It is your presence that is most important.

One may forget words, but the way one feels can never easily be forgotten.

When I was at the precipice

And I had reached my very limit

And couldn't tolerate my reality any longer

The Universe rewarded me with exactly what I needed.

It reciprocated the purity of the heart I possessed indeed

When everything and everyone, and even I, were failing me

My saving grace came in the form of two little beings.

The love I received was in their constant requests to see me.

For those two, I saw the need to continue to fight to stay alive

Because of their growing demand to see me every time

I was made to see the light from a different sunshine

That even the slightest reminder of it brightens my soul

As I continue to venture through my darkest days.

Thirty-Nine

The Greatest Magi/Alchemist

If you allow your emotions to rule your life, they will ruin your life even though they influence your life.

The Universe doesn't operate from a state of emotion, but responds to your every feeling of creation that is backed by your raw emotions. It reciprocates whatever you give by reflecting and magnifying it.

The life force that is within you is a great magnet. Your outward reality is an inward reflection of your deepest thoughts, both consciously and sublime.

And the perpetuation of your thoughts becomes your subconscious truths. And your subconscious mind is the one responsible for manifesting your reality. For it is constantly recording and at work for you.

People always want something to believe in, yet it is most difficult for many to believe in themselves.

The greatest alchemist is he who can transmute negativity into positivity and can turn a negative situation into a positive reality.

The greatest sets of breakthroughs are often the outward triumphs and reflections of the innermost pain felt. This is why most are overwhelmed with tears of joy after overcoming, achieving and rising to the occasion.

Therefore, see how pointless envy and jealousy become when in comparison to the discovery of the profound truths hidden in plain sight.

The mystery of the Universe is written and encoded in energy. To decode it will require you to increase your vibration and overall frequency.

Love will quickly get you there, and Gratitude will most definitely keep you there. Love and gratitude are the highest frequencies.

Forty

The Power Of Stillness

When you learn to be focused and still in mind at the same time,

That's when you become perfectly in tune with the ever-eternal and Highest Force possible.

This Most High Divine Force only appears to be still, not because IT is always present and constant

But because IT is moving faster than any sense of perception can even begin to fathom.

Your ego no longer places a time on expectations, because stillness in mind practices divine timing.

The more still you become, the faster your manifestations become your everyday reality.

It isn't easy to trust the process all the time.

But remain focused and meditate with the power of stillness, and you will see clearly and be able to find.

That it is all in your mind.

AFTERWORD FROM THE AUTHOR

When you align yourself with the trinity about yourself, the entire Universe willingly conspires with you.

The trinity that is to be aligned with you consists of one, your human consciousness/awareness; two, your subconscious mind and third; your Spirit/Higher Self.

Your subconscious mind is the recorder of your every imagination, visualisation, thought, word, action, vision, dream, and so much more. Yet it is the source that manifests your reality through the signature of your most dominant emotions and feelings of creation, as well as the consistency of your overall energy pattern.

It is also a great transmitter and receiver of information to and from the Universe. It is also the point where you can communicate back and forth with your Higher Self, once you learn to silence the rambunctiousness of the carnal mind effectively.

The only thing that separates you from the trinity about yourself is when you choose to vibrate at low frequencies. This misalignment takes the form of fear, hatred, ingratitude, envy and jealousy, pessimism, overthinking, and constant negativity, to name a few.

Also, the things we choose to consume are not just physical, but also mental and visual. Assured alignment comes through constant love and gratitude. Also, forgiveness of self and others, as it lightens the mind and elevates your overall frequency. Yet not forgetting the many valuable lessons taught.

When you're in perfect alignment with yourself, your emotions are nothing more than tools to be used. You would learn to think less from an emotional state and more from an intellectual standpoint.

Emotions are like fuel that drives you, but intellect gives you access to the steering wheel. You can either utilise them effectively or be utilised inefficiently. Such are the two options available to everyone.

Power minus control leads to catastrophic imprisonment; Power plus control leads to equilibrium, the very source of freedom.

Tevin C. R. Dubé

8th April, 2020

Trinidad and Tobago

ACKNOWLEDGEMENT

I dedicate this effort to my mother, KathyAnn Marie Toppin. You're the reason for it all.

To Le'Shanae for simply giving me so much-needed encouragement and inspiration that made me pick up the pen after an eight-month hiatus during the COVID-19 pandemic.

To Makhaya and Kieron, who divinely motivate me through the highest order of simplicity and their genuinely affectionate nature towards me. Blessings, I never knew I would have needed one day to come into my life.

To my uncle Nigel and my true spiritual brother Keion—Thank you both for standing strong alongside me during this test of time.

To Andy and Jamal, thank you both for being pivotal and crucial in helping me with my most recent artworks. The Universe shall always be favourable to you both.

To you, my beloved and cherished reader, may you reap the fullest rewards of the many positive vibrations bequeathed unto you. May the Universal Key be unlocked within yourself so that you may access your fullest potential.

ABOUT AUTHOR

Tevin is truly a prolific writer, as his works speak for themselves. His life is truly a source of inspiration from his early childhood to the present.

He is not only one of a kind but the first of his kind in more ways than one. He is most definitely redefining the meaning of success with an impregnable drive and indomitable display of 'willpower'.

Tevin is constantly evolving as he keeps rising to and above the occasion. Even though he is soaring higher and higher every time, he is still nowhere near the pinnacle of his successes or what he is yet to accomplish.

He is now an official author of 8 books, all published within 4 years, by his own call. Tevin is a gem to be cherished and a national treasure to be beheld. He will definitely be written up in the history books as a unique writer with a universal display of wisdom and a master wordsmith. He will be dubbed one of the greatest writers of all time.

Books By The Author

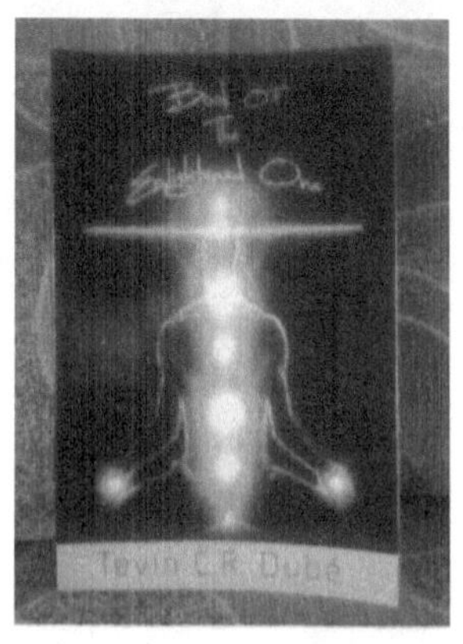

Book Of The Enlightened One

Amen: A Great Light Within

Divine Darkness

The Mystery Behind Life,

Death And Resurrection

A Silent Truth

Psalms From A New King David

SELF

Attract Abundance: Learn

How To Live Abundantly

9 789769 633445